SALLY'S STREAM, 1985

THE LIGHT OF IRELAND

BY RON ROSENSTOCK

IN DECEMBER 1971, I ARRIVED AT SHANNON AIRPORT on my first visit to Ireland. Driving north from the airport, I experienced remarkable changes in weather and corresponding changes in the light. At first, the sun gleamed in a brilliant sky. Suddenly the wind began to blow and heavy gray clouds gathered overhead. Within minutes, rain blurred the greens of the land with the gray of the sky. The rain intensified and without warning, hail pelted down with a fury.

But as quickly as it started, the hail stopped and the rain changed into a gentle mist. How soft the light seemed then. The air was clean and sweet with the smells of plants and wet earth. As the storm passed, the sky grew brighter. Moments later, the sun appeared and everything glistened. Within that thirty minutes, Ireland gave me a glimpse of her treasures. All at once I knew I was entering into a long and important relationship with this rare and beautiful country. My love for Ireland has spanned almost thirty years. I continue to be inspired by what the light and the landscape reveal.

This book of photographs represents my feelings for Ireland and the discoveries I have made there. It is my hope that in some way, the creative spirit in all of us will be awakened by Ireland's beauty and inspire us to protect such treasures of nature.

The Light of Ireland

PHOTOGRAPHS BY RON ROSENSTOCK

THE PHOTOGRAPHY OF RON ROSENSTOCK

BY PAUL CAPONIGRO

RON HAS WORKED WITHIN THE TRADITION of large-format landscape photography for many years and comes to it with caring and a simple love of the craft. His eye surveys the external world as if inquiring; his images offer us intimations of answers. The elements of his subjects seem to align themselves to his quiet intent. Cloud, water, stone, and mist-drenched and sun-gleamed flora arrange themselves in his photographs much like iron filings aligning to a magnet. Within this realm of affirmation we hear the quiet "whisperings" of his silver manipulations. His revelations, and our own, soon follow.

Ron's images not only convey the grace of a fine tradition but also his gratitude to those masters of photography who provided him with a foundation in the value of the craft. His photographs bespeak the peace and poise that come from attuning himself to the medium and to his own world. What appears to be a longing in Ron's photographs mirrors the longing we all feel for the spirit concealed from view. Mystery seems to be gentle with Ron; he accepts the challenge of discovery without brooding excessively over veiled treasures. Through the camera he sustains his search for connections with such mysteries. We see in his photographs his perseverance towards the greater flight.

1. THREE TREES, DOO LOUGH, COUNTY MAYO, 1975

2. STANDING STONE, ACHILL ISLAND, 1971

3. SILVER STRAND, COUNTY MAYO, 1980

4. WMEELREA MOUNTAINS, COUNTY MAYO, 1985

5. DOO LOUGH REFLECTIONS, COUNTY MAYO, 1975

6. THATCHED COTTAGE, COUNTY MAYO, 1975

7. Single Cloud, Clare Island, County Mayo, 1981

8. SILVER STREAM, THALLABAWN, COUNTY MAYO, 1979

9. BUNOWEN BEACH, COUNTY MAYO, 1979

10. ASHLEEM BAY, ACHILL ISLAND, 1983

11. SUNSET AT SHEEFFREY, COUNTY MAYO, 1985

12. CLARE ISLAND, COUNTY MAYO, 1981

13. TIDE POOLS, DOWN PATRICK HEAD, COUNTY MAYO, 1992

14. CLEARING SKY, THALLABAWN, COUNTY MAYO, 1979

15. BRANCH AND TIDE, BUNOWEN BEACH, COUNTY MAYO, 1981

16. BALLINAHINCH LOUGH, COUNTY GALWAY, 1992

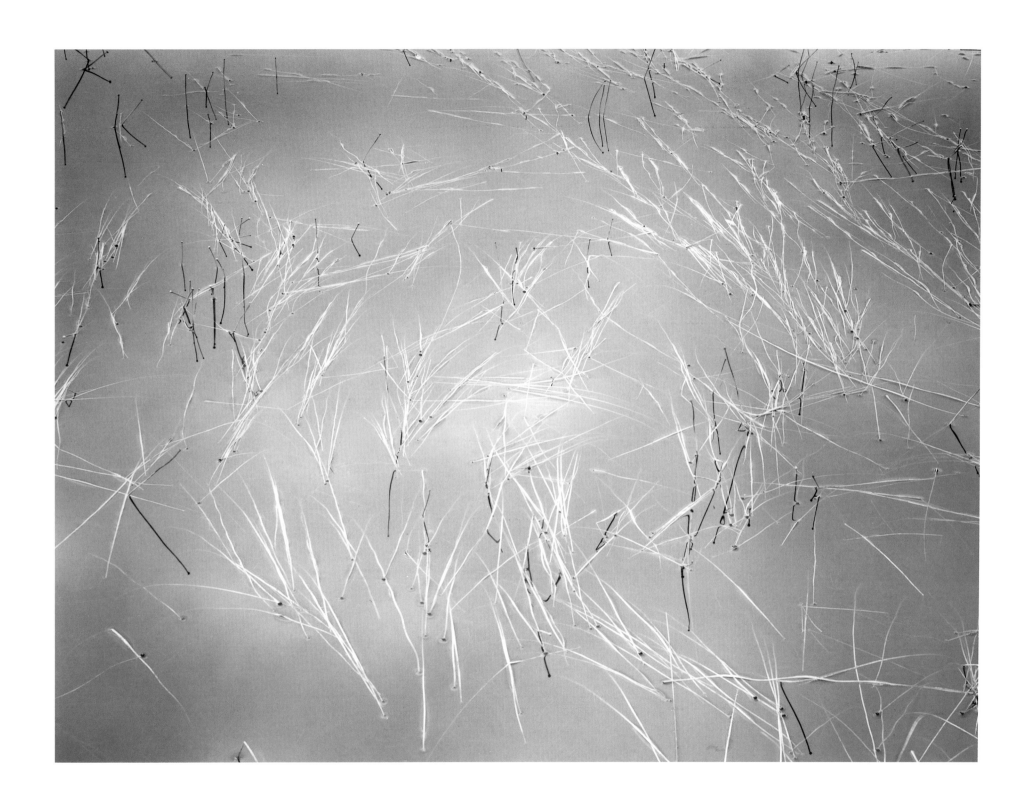

17. WATER REEDS AT CONG, COUNTY MAYO, 1986

18. THREE FALLS, COUNTY KERRY, 1976

19. DOOEGA, ACHILL ISLAND, COUNTY MAYO, 1985

20. VINE AND FERN, SHEEFFREY, COUNTY MAYO, 1991

21. SHEEFFREY WOOD, COUNTY MAYO, 1986

22. STONE CIRCLE, SHEEFFREY, COUNTY MAYO, 1986

23. GUBBAUN POINT, COUNTY MAYO, 1972

24. KEEM STRAND, ACHILL ISLAND, 1996

25. SILVER LEAF, STREAMSTOWN, COUNTY MAYO, 1997

RON ROSENSTOCK

CURRICULUM VITAE

Born: 1943, Monticello, New York

Education: Goddard College 1976-1977 M.A. (Photography)
Boston University 1965-1968 A.A. (History)

1969-71 Private studies with Paul Caponigro.

1968 Participated in the study group, "Consciousness in Photography," conducted by Minor White.

1967 Participated in the workshop, "Vision and the Man Behind the Camera," conducted by Minor White.

Solo Exhibitions:

2000 *CHIOSTRO: Images of Italy by Ron Rosenstock,* Jewish Community Center Gallery, Worcester, Massachusetts

1999 *Green: A Photo Essay in Black and White,* Altamira Contemporary Arts and Crafts Gallery, Islip, New York
Ron Rosenstock, Photographs, Fletcher/Priest Gallery, Worcester, Massachusetts

1998 *The Light of Ireland,* Schabes Gallery, Chicago, Illinois
Sacred Places, Holden Gale Free Library, Holden, Massachusetts

1997 *One Earth,* Center for Contemporary Arts, Abilene, Texas
One Earth, Schabes Gallery, Chicago, Illinois
Photographs of Mayo, Waterfront Gallery, Westport, County Mayo, Ireland

1996 *Glimpses of a Secret Ireland,* Arabella Grand Hotel Gallery, Frankfurt, Germany
Ireland, Schabes Gallery, Chicago, Illinois
New Work, The Gallery at Atlantic Filmworks, Hamden, Connecticut

1995 *Sanctuary,* Worcester Center for Crafts Gallery, Worcester, Massachusetts

1994 *Ron Rosenstock, Photographer,* Bryant Library Gallery, Roslyn, New York

1993 *Photographs by Ron Rosenstock,* Geoghegan Gallery of Photography, Galway, Ireland

1991 *Studies in Light,* Fitchburg Art Museum, Fitchburg, Massachusetts
Photographs of Kenya and Ecuador by Ron Rosenstock, Atlantic Filmworks, Hamden, Connecticut
Sea Marks, Foothills Theater, Worcester, Massachusetts

1990 *Photographs of Ireland,* The Gallery at Atlantic Filmworks, Hamden, Connecticut

1989 *African Rhythm/Irish Cadence,* Ledel Gallery, New York, New York
Black and White Landscapes, Geoghegan Gallery of Photography, Galway, Ireland
Photographs by Ron Rosenstock, Saint Marks School, Southboro, Massachusetts

1988 *Trees Are Poems That The Earth Writes To The Sky,* Newton Library Gallery, Newton, Massachusetts

1987 *Fifteen Years of Ireland in Black and White,* Grace O'Malley Art Gallery, Westport, County Mayo, Ireland
Ron Rosenstock, Photographs, University of Massachusetts Medical School, Worcester, Massachusetts

1986 *Photographs of Ireland,* Gordon Library, Worcester Polytechnic Institute, Worcester, Massachusetts

1985 *Photographs by Ron Rosenstock,* Walt Kuhn Gallery, Cape Neddick, Maine

1984 *Developments in Lights,* Clark University, Worcester, Massachusetts
Ireland, Photographs by Ron Rosenstock, Irish Tourist Board, New York, New York
Ron Rosenstock, Lawrence Academy, Groton, Massachusetts

1982 *New Work,* Front Street Gallery, Wilmington, Delaware
Ron Rosenstock, Louisiana State University, Baton Rouge, Louisiana

1981 *Ron Rosenstock,* Darkroom Gallery, Denver, Colorado

1980 *Ireland,* Front Street Gallery, Wilmington, Delaware
Ireland, Photographs by Ron Rosenstock, Clark University, Worcester, Massachusetts
Photographs by Ron Rosenstock, Gallery of Photography, Dublin, Ireland
Photographs by Ron Rosenstock, Saint Marks School, Southboro, Massachusetts

1979 *Photographs by Ron Rosenstock,* Education Centre, Castlebar, County Mayo, Ireland
Photographs by Ron Rosenstock, Photo Graphic Workshop, New Canaan, Connecticut

1978 *Photographs by Ron Rosenstock,* University of Massachusetts Medical School, Worcester, Massachusetts

1977 *Photographs by Ron Rosenstock,* Carpenter Center, Harvard University, Cambridge, Massachusetts

(Solo Exhibitions, continued)

1976   *Photographs by Ron Rosenstock,* Bartlett Gallery, Atlantic Union College, South Lancaster, Massachusetts

1974   *Photographs by Ron Rosenstock,* Thoor Ballylee Museum, Gort, County Galway, Ireland
Photographs by Ron Rosenstock, First Congregational Church, Northboro, Massachusetts

1973   *Ron Rosenstock, 8x10 Contacts,* Creative Photography Gallery, Massachusetts Institute of Technology, Cambridge, Massachusetts

1971   *Photographs by Ron Rosenstock,* Experiment Gallery, Holden, Massachusetts
Photographs by Ron Rosenstock, Bancroft School, Worcester, Massachusetts

1970   *Photographs by Ron Rosenstock,* Cary Library, Lexington, Massachusetts

1969   *A Way to Look at Things,* Worcester Craft Center, Worcester, Massachusetts

Group Exhibitions:

1999   *Fifth Annual Collectors' Print Auction,* Texas Photographic Society, San Antonio, Texas *Irish Artists Night,* Tweed's, Worcester, Massachusetts
One Earth, Two Views: Photographs by Stephen DiRado and Ron Rosenstock, Clark University, Worcester, Massachusetts
Ron Rosenstock, Photographs; James Tellin Wood Constructions, Fletcher/Priest Gallery, Worcester, Massachusetts

1998   *Northeast Nature and Wildlife Expo,* Providence, Rhode Island

1995   *Paul Caponigro, Ron Rosenstock: Spiritual Landscapes,* Fletcher/Priest Gallery, Worcester, Massachusetts

1991   *Tree,* Clark University, Worcester, Massachusetts

1990   *Caponigro/Rosenstock/Stettner,* Neikrug Gallery, New York, New York
Photographic Landscapes, Wenniger Graphics, Provincetown, Massachusetts

1989   *ARTS Worcester Revisited,* Cultural Assembly Gallery, Worcester Center, Worcester, Massachusetts
Caponigro/Rosenstock, Gay Head Gallery, Martha's Vineyard, Massachusetts
Fools Gold, Bridge Mills Gallery, Galway, Ireland
Fools Gold, City Centre, Dublin, Ireland
Keepers of Light, Collectors Gallery, Worcester, Massachusetts

1985   *Landscape II: Cole Weston, Lilliane DeCock, Ron Rosenstock,* Images Gallery, Cincinnati, Ohio
(Untitled), Walt Kuhn Gallery, Cape Neddick, Maine
Westport Artists, Westport Arts Center, Westport, County Mayo, Ireland

1983   *ARTS Worcester,* Juried Art Exhibition, Cultural Assembly Gallery, Worcester Art Museum, Worcester, Massachusetts
Irish Visions, Worcester Craft Center, Worcester, Massachusetts
Tradition and Experiment, Bartlett Gallery, Atlantic Union College, South Lancaster, Massachusetts

1982   *Faculty Exhibit,* Clark University, Worcester, Massachusetts
Ireland, Ledel Gallery, New York, New York

1981   *Summer Show,* Images Gallery, Cincinnati, Ohio

1980   *Photoways — Twelve New England Photographers,* Clark University, Worcester, Massachusetts
Polaroid Collection, Recent Acquisitions, Clarence Kennedy Gallery, Cambridge, Massachusetts

1978   *Collection of the Worcester Art Museum,* Worcester Art Museum, Worcester, Massachusetts
Faculty Show, Worcester Craft Center, Worcester, Massachusetts
The Irish Photographic Workshop, Bartlett Gallery, Atlantic Union College, South Lancaster, Massachusetts

1977   *Four Directions,* Worcester Craft Center, Worcester, Massachusetts
25th Anniversary Show, Worcester Craft Center, Worcester, Massachusetts

1976   *Members' Exhibit,* Friends of Photography, Carmel, California

1973   *Faculty Show,* Worcester Craft Center, Worcester, Massachusetts
Worcester Area Photographers, Lieutenant Governor's Office, Boston, Massachusetts

1972   *Faculty Show,* Worcester Craft Center, Worcester, Massachusetts

1971   *Faculty Show,* Dana Hall School, Wellesley, Massachusetts

1970   *Area Show,* Worcester Art Museum, Worcester, Massachusetts
Innermost House, Massachusetts Institute of Technology, Cambridge, Massachusetts

1969   *Eleventh Rhode Island Arts Festival,* Providence, Rhode Island
Fourteen Photographers, Schenectady Art Museum, Schenectady, New York

1968   *Light 7,* Curated by Minor White, Massachusetts Institute of Technology, Cambridge, Massachusetts
Second Sight, Worcester Craft Center, Worcester, Massachusetts
Tenth Rhode Island Arts Festival, Providence, Rhode Island
Twelve Photographers, Massachusetts Institute of Technology, Cambridge, Massachusetts

Permanent Collections:

Castlebar Urban District Council, Castlebar, County Mayo, Ireland
The Fogg Art Museum, Harvard University, Cambridge, Massachusetts
International Center of Photography, New York, New York
Massachusetts Institute of Technology, Cambridge, Massachusetts
Polaroid Corporation, Cambridge, Massachusetts
Torre Guelfa Hotel, Florence, Italy
University of Arizona, Tucson, Arizona
University of New Mexico, Albuquerque, New Mexico
Villa Rosa Gallery, San Leolino, Italy
The Worcester Art Museum, Worcester, Massachusetts

Corporate Sales:

Aware Corporation, Bedford, Massachusetts
Fidelity Investments, Boston, Massachusetts

Private Collections:

Maeve Binchy
Paul Caponigro
Deepak Chopra
Catherine Steinmann

Portfolios:

1997   *Light of Ireland,* Portfolio II, privately issued limited edition
1975   *Light of Ireland,* Portfolio I, privately issued limited edition

Published Works:

Articles, Books, Media Productions, Reviews

1999   *The Landmark,* Holden, Massachusetts, October 14, pp.1,34.

1997   *The Literary Review,* Fairleigh Dickinson University, Summer 1997, Volume 40, Number 4, Cover Photograph and pp.650-654.
View Camera, July/August, pp.22-28.

1995   *Canon Photo Safari,* four half-hour cable television productions.
Worcester Sunday Telegram, April 2, Datebook, pp.11,15. Review/Interview.

1994   *Channel 11, Community Access Television*, Interview.
Fánaíocht I gContae Mhaigh Eo (Rambles in County Mayo), Seamus Uidhir with 70 photographs by Ron Rosenstock. Dublin, Ireland: An Gum.
Newsday, July 29, Section B, Review, p.34.

1993   *Ireland of the Welcomes,* Dublin, Ireland. Volume 42, Number 2, pp.26-29.
The New York Times, June 20, Travel Section, pp.1,19.

1992   *Channel 11, Community Access Television,* Interview.
Worth Magazine, August/September, pp.128-129.

1991   *View Camera,* May/June, Interview, pp.3-10.

1990   *Channel 11, Community Access Television*, Interview.
International Center of Photography Annual Report, from their collection, p.44.
The Basics of Black and White Photography, Videotape I.
The New York Times, July 15, Travel Section, pp.1, 15, 16.
The Zone System, Videotape II.

1989   *American Photographers, An Illustrated Who's Who Among Leading Contemporary Americans,* Facts on File, pp.251-252.
Vineyard Gazette, Martha's Vineyard, Massachusetts, May 26.
Wachusett People, pp.1,6-7.
Worcester Magazine, p.20.

1988   *The New York Times,* Travel Section, pp.1, 21, 39.

1982-85   *Druid Calendar,* Cahill and Co., Dobbs Ferry, New York.

1979   *Ireland of the Welcomes,* Dublin, Ireland, Volume 28, Number 4, July/August, pp.30-32.

1977   *Photography: The Portrait,* privately issued limited edition monograph, each with eight original prints.

1972   *Camera,* Lucerne, Switzerland, July, pp.14-23.

1971   *Camera,* Lucerne, Switzerland, April, pp.20-21,25,38.

1970   *Camera,* Lucerne, Switzerland, June, pp.36,37,40.

1968   *Aperture,* Volume 1, Number 2, "Light 7," p.9.

Workshops and Lectures:

Ongoing   *Irish Photographic Workshops,* two-week workshops for photographers of all levels and formats, seven to ten workshops per year, March through October, Westport, County Mayo, Ireland. Host, leader and instructor. 1976 through present.
Tuscany/Venice Photographic Workshops, two-to-three week workshops for photographers of all levels and formats, one to three times per year, leader and instructor. 1993 through present.
The Sunday Night Group, a group of advanced photographers who work independently, then meet with me to share their work. 1970 through present.
Annual Lecture, Castlebar Camera Club, Castlebar, County Mayo, Ireland

2000   *Peru Photographic Workshop,* two-week workshop for photographers of all levels and formats, leader and instructor

1999   *Nepal and Photographic Workshop,* two-week workshop for photographers of all levels and formats, leader and instructor

1997   *Nepal and India Photographic Workshop,* three-week workshop for photographers of all levels and formats, leader and instructor
Southwest Photographic Workshop, two-week workshop for photographers of all levels and formats, leader and instructor

1996   *New Zealand Photographic Workshop,* two-week workshop for photographers of all levels and formats, leader and instructor
Peru Photographic Workshop, two-week workshop for photographers of all levels and formats, leader and instructor

1995   *Nepal Photographic Workshop,* two-week workshop for photographers of all levels and formats, leader and instructor

1994   *New Zealand Photographic Workshop,* two-week workshop for photographers of all levels and formats, leader and instructor

1993   *Large Format Workshop,* Geoghegan Gallery of Photography, Galway, Ireland, lecturer

1990-93   *Ecuador/Amazon Basin/Galapagos Islands Photographic Workshop,* three-week workshops for photographers of all levels and formats, one trip per year, leader and instructor

(Workshops and Lectures, continued)

1989   *Beginning Photography,* Humanities Class, Wachusett Regional High School, Holden, Massachusetts, lecturer
Large Format Workshop, Geoghegan Gallery of Photography, Galway, Ireland, lecturer

1988   *Irish Photographic Workshop,* two-week workshop for photographers of all levels and formats, conducted with visiting artist Paul Caponigro
Kenya Photographic Workshops, two-week workshops for photographers of all levels and formats, two tours, leader and instructor

1986   *Instant Slide Film,* Polaroid Corporation, Cambridge, Massachusetts, lecturer

Faculty Appointments:

Ongoing   Instructor, Beginning Photography and Advanced Photography, Clark University, Worcester, Massachusetts. 1974 to present.

1976-79   Instructor, Beginning Photography and Advanced Photography, Bancroft School, Worcester, Massachusetts

1969-72   Instructor, Advance Photography, Dana Hall School, Wellesley, Massachusetts

1968-79   Instructor, Beginning, Intermediate and Advanced Photography, Worcester Craft Center, Worcester, Massachusetts

Additional Experience:

1980-82   Member of the Polaroid Collection, Cambridge, Massachusetts

1972   Consultant in Photography Department for Old Sturbridge Village, Sturbridge, Massachusetts

1967-70   Architectural photographer for the Architects' Collaborative, Cambridge, Massachusetts; Acorn Structures, Concord, Massachusetts; and Kubitz and Pepi, Wellesley, Massachusetts

1966-68   Freelance photographer for Houghton Mifflin, Textbook Division, Boston, Massachusetts

1966-67   Darkroom technician, Boston University, Boston, Massachusetts

Memberships:

Ongoing   Member, Cultural Advisory Board, Bancroft School, Worcester, Massachusetts. 1995 to present.
Member, Cultural Arts Committee, Worcester Jewish Community Center, Worcester, Massachusetts, 1997 to present.

Awards and Honors:

1998   *Black and White Category, Best in Show,* Northeast Nature and Wildlife Expo, Providence, Rhode Island

1995   *Honorary Citizen of Westport,* Westport Town Council, Westport, County Mayo, Ireland

1983   *First Prize in Photography,* ARTS Worcester, Juried Art Exhibition, Cultural Assembly of Greater Worcester and the Worcester Art Museum, Worcester, Massachusetts

Web Sites:

Photography Workshops:
    Voyagers International, http://www.voyagers.com
Photography Galleries:
    http://www.earthlightgallery.com
    http://www.naturegallery.com
    http://www.pascarelligallery.com
    http://www.planetpoint.com
    http://www.ronrosenstock.com
    http://www.neart.com

ISBN 0-615-11218-8

Copyright 2000 by Ron Rosenstock
Published by The Silver Strand Press
91 Sunnyside Avenue, Holden, Massachusetts 01520

Duotone Printing by Mercantile/Image Press Inc.
West Boylston, Massachusetts

Type Set in Adobe Garamond
Printed on Potlatch McCoy 100# Gloss Text
Typography by CatsEye Graphics, Worcester, Massachusetts